Original title:
Waves of Tranquility

Copyright © 2025 Creative Arts Management OÜ
All rights reserved.

Author: Natalia Harrington
ISBN HARDBACK: 978-1-80581-645-4
ISBN PAPERBACK: 978-1-80581-172-5
ISBN EBOOK: 978-1-80581-645-4

Nature's Heartbeat Along the Shore

Seagulls squawk in silly flight,
Chasing crabs with all their might.
The tide rolls in and out, just so,
While fish debate who's 'making waves' below.

Shells wear hats, a sandy style,
Starfish twirl, they dance awhile.
The shoreline whispers, 'What a show!',
As surfboards wobble, all aglow.

Daydreams Adrift in Sapphire

Bubbles rise in goofy glee,
A dolphin laughs, as wild as can be.
Beach balls bounce with all their flair,
While the tide performs its sandy care.

Seashells gossip, oh what news!
Fish wear t-shirts, sun-soaked hues.
Crabs in sunglasses stroll the sand,
With flip-flops on, they're feeling grand.

Cradled by Coastal Embrace

Kites fly high, a vibrant dance,
While seaweed sways like it's in a trance.
The tide's a friend, a jolly mate,
As sea cucumbers speculate their fate.

Jellyfish bounce with jelly joy,
While kids build castles, oh what a ploy!
They claim it's fort, but really it's fun,
As waves peek in, saying, 'Not just anyone!'

Serenity Wrapped in Ocean's Cloth

Mermaids giggle, their hair a mess,
As crabs nap soundly, feeling blessed.
The ocean sighs a gentle tune,
While rubber duckies float past the moon.

Seagulls play tag in the sunny sky,
Sandcastles sway, oh me, oh my!
With every splash, a joyous cheer,
In playful jests, we hold them dear.

The Dance of Soft Ripples

Tiny splashes prance with glee,
While fishy friends swim carelessly.
Seagulls squawk a silly tune,
Pretending they're a dancing boon.

Bubbles rise like jokes in air,
Playing hide and seek with flair.
Shimmering shimmer, oh so bright,
Even crabs do the cha-cha right!

Serenity Beneath the Horizon

Under the sun, a cheerful glow,
Where sunscreens rule and tan lines grow.
Old beach chairs that creak and sigh,
As seagulls dive and sandwiches fly.

Coolers filled with snacks untold,
Crispy chips that never get old.
The sand's a comedic little friend,
Tickling toes till laughter blends.

Ocean's Lullaby at Dusk

As twilight whispers, off they fall,
Beach balls rolling, having a ball.
Flip-flops flop, a toe-tapping beat,
As sunsets blend with laughter sweet.

The crabs hold a beach party, oh my!
They dance with gusto and no need to try.
Shells holding secrets from long ago,
Join the revelry, rowdy and slow.

Horizon's Embrace of Stillness

The horizon stretches with a grin,
Where doodling dolphins always win.
They paint the sky with silly arcs,
While sunbathers nap like tired sharks.

Laughter bubbles from fishy cheers,
Mermaids gossip, spreading good cheers.
In this stillness, smiles take flight,
With giggles echoing into the night.

Embraces of the Evening Tide

The sun dips low with a zesty grin,
Fish throw parties with splashes and spins.
Seagulls swoop down with a taco in tow,
Even crabs join in for a wobbly show.

Bubbles pop up, like jokes on the sea,
Shells share secrets, like laughter set free.
The moon starts to chuckle, shining so bright,
As starfish do yoga, a marvelous sight.

The Lull of Ocean's Embrace

A dolphin in pajamas takes a cozy float,
While jellyfish dance with a whimsical coat.
The tide hums a tune, a lullaby cheer,
As seaweed sways, with a wiggle in here.

The crabs are all dressed in their finest of shells,
Trading old stories filled with fishy spells.
The anchovies giggle, doing flips all around,
In this grand aquatic circus, joy unbound.

Tranquil Currents Beneath the Stars

Anchors aweigh, let the night take the stage,
The ocean's a book, with each wave a page.
Starfish tell tales of their journeys afar,
While plankton recite poems under the stars.

The sunflowers bob, in a dance that's sublime,
As sandpipers prance, playing tag with the time.
Each ripple will giggle, a joyous delight,
And fish wear tuxedos for the dance tonight.

Stillness Awaits on Water's Edge

A hermit crab fumbles, ties shoes that are tight,
Sand castles giggle, of glares from the kite.
The tide rolls in with a snicker and glee,
As seashells compete in their own little spree.

A picnic of snacks spills all over the shore,
Fish bring the salsa, while octopus stirs.
The breeze lends a hand, pulling pranks so divine,
As the sun waves goodnight—what a funny design!

Secrets Hidden in Shallow Waters

The beachball floats, a curious sight,
Fish giggle as they dart with delight.
Beach shovels lie with a wink and a grin,
Next to the sandcastles, we'll never win.

Shells whisper tales of octopus dreams,
Mermaids chuckle in the sun's golden beams.
We build and we break, oh what a fun mess,
At the edge of the tide, we just must confess.

The Quiet Embrace of Dusk

As the sun dips low, the sky's in a twist,
Seagulls are planning their evening tryst.
Sand licked by shadows, a grand masquerade,
While crabs practice tango, oh what a parade!

Dusk dresses all in a rosy-hued gown,
And laughter rings loud as we settle down.
With snacks in our hands, a picnic in tow,
Even the stars can't help but glow.

Sand and Sea's Whispered Secrets

Footprints lead measures of silly retreat,
As flip-flops squeak with each frolicsome beat.
Buckets of dreams filled with laughter and fun,
A crab gives a wave, to declare he has won.

Tides giggle softly, a pulse in the night,
Ice cream melts faster, but what a sweet sight!
Sandy dog dashes with zeal and grace,
Leaving paw prints like a clumsy embrace.

Reflections of a Tranquil Mind

A calm ocean surface, a mirror for sprites,
Who dance with the clouds and giggle in heights.
The laughter of kids tumbles over the shore,
While time drifts away, who could want more?

So we build little castles, our dreams made of sand,
As waves tell us secrets, our feet in the strand.
The evening embraces, a cozy delight,
While tiny fish snicker at the moon's silver light.

Undercurrents of Reflection

Bubbles rise to greet my toes,
They giggle as the current flows.
Sun hats dance on the shore so bright,
Sandy friends join in delight.

A crab in shades, what a sight!
He struts his stuff, oh what a fright.
Shells whisper secrets from the deep,
While starfish plans put me to sleep.

With each splish, a silly claim,
Fish gossip spreads—a bubbling game.
The tide pulls jokes and sandy winks,
I laugh so hard, it makes me think!

In this vast world, we all just float,
On inflatable ducks that seem to gloat.
With beach balls bouncing near my head,
I ponder life and laugh instead.

A Still Journey Over the Waves

Sailing seats on floating logs,
We paddle past the swimming frogs.
Ice cream drips, a sticky plight,
Seagulls steal snacks—what a bite!

Our raft it wobbles, giggles fly,
As I spill juice, oh my, oh my!
Under the sun, we drift so slow,
While dolphins dance in an awkward show.

Flip-flops slap like silly fish,
In search of treasure, we make a wish.
A sunburned nose, bright as a rose,
Keeps my friends guessing—who's in the throes?

As evening falls, we spot a lighthouse,
Its beam makes me feel like a mouse.
With a laugh and a wave, we call it a day,
In the amusing chase of life's playful play.

Ethereal Calm Under Twilight's Veil

Under the stars, I try to dream,
But a seagull's squawk bursts the theme.
With cocoa in hand, I gaze at the night,
The moon grins back, oh what a sight!

Shadows of crabs scuttle away,
Prancing merrily, they seem to play.
A hammock sways but snags a toe,
Which makes me laugh for all to know.

In this peaceful hush, my thoughts carouse,
As tidal whispers tease the souse.
Fireflies glow with a jazzy beat,
While I shuffle my feet to the rhythm of heat.

With every splash, my worries cease,
The ocean giggles, offering peace.
As laughter glides on the cool night air,
I find serenity in this joyful affair.

Heartbeats Lost in the Sea's Ululation

Heartbeat racing with each loud wave,
A jellyfish dances, what a brave knave!
I bob along with a goofy grin,
Splashing around, let the fun begin.

A whale's deep chuckle bounces around,
While gulls join in, making my heart pound.
Tangled in seaweed, I do a jig,
With fishy companions, we get real big.

Seashells sing a cheerful tune,
As dolphins play like mischievous goons.
My snorkel's fogged, I try to boast,
While squids shoot ink, now that's the most!

In this frothy whirl, I lose my cares,
Giggles and splashes fill the warm airs.
A chorus of fun, in ocean's embrace,
We find pure delight in this playful space.

The Gentle Touch of Distant Shores

The sun reclines on lazy backs,
Seagulls giggle at sailor's hacks.
A crab in shades struts with flair,
While fish all laugh, they've lost their hair.

A turtle snores on sandy dunes,
Counting all the silly tunes.
The sandcastles lean, then they fall,
As giggling kids start the free-for-all.

A clam winks at the passing tide,
"Don't worry, mate, I've got some pride!"
With shells and snickers all around,
The ocean hosts a jolly sound.

And when the evening curtains fall,
Starfish cheer in a coral hall.
The night brings jokes from fishes true,
As crabs retell the tales anew.

Resting Souls of the Ocean Bed

In depths where seaweed hums a tune,
The flounder dreams of being a moon.
An octopus juggles with delight,
Saying, "Hey guys, check out my tight!"

The clams take selfies on the sand,
While whispers weave a playful band.
A starfish strikes a model's pose,
Ignoring the jellyfish's doze.

Down below where currents flow,
A hidden dolphin paints with glow.
"I swear I'm an artist!" it laughs,
As bubbles create quirky gaffes.

The seaweed shakes in giggly glee,
As crabs attempt the limbo spree.
With every splash, a chuckle fades,
The ocean's joy in tidal shades.

Spirit of the Moonlit Waters

Under the glow of silly stars,
A fish in glasses hums to guitars.
The waves jive, singing silly songs,
As turtles groove, rights to their wrongs.

A hermit crab with boots so bright,
Starts a dance party every night.
The shrimp throw confetti in the air,
While the seahorses whip their hair!

At midnight's call, the dolphins cheer,
"Join us, friends, let's spread the cheer!"
They spin and twirl in moonbeam glow,
Making waves all put on a show.

And when the sun begins to rise,
The ocean sighs with sleepy eyes.
But come next dusk, without a doubt,
The playful spirit will come out.

Captured Blue in Stillness

In the calm where laughter meets the breeze,
A fish puts on its best of freeze.
"Look at me!" it shouts in glee,
As seaweed whispers, "Let it be."

The bubbles giggle, float, and pop,
Each wave a prank that never stops.
A clownfish jokes with every flip,
While the anchor fish takes a dip.

The skies above envy the fun,
As the seashells bask in the sun.
Every bob and tilt tells a tale,
In the silence where they prevail.

The tides may change, the breezes blow,
But in their dance, the humor flows.
With every hue of ocean's hue,
A gentle smile is born anew.

The Calm Between the Currents

In a sea where no one swims,
A fish just wrote some silly hymns.
He joked with crabs and played some games,
But dreamt of jelly, far too lame.

Seagulls laughing on the shore,
Spotted a clam who wanted more.
"Hey buddy, life's a bit too slow!"
The clam replied, "It's not the show!"

A turtle danced in sunlit glee,
While dolphins served him cups of tea.
With swirling pastries, not so glum,
Imagination made them hum.

So if you seek a funny sight,
Just watch the ocean's playful bite.
Between the currents, don't you fret,
There's laughter waiting—no regret.

Reflections in a Quiet Sea

Bubbles popped like little jokes,
While anchovies entertained folks.
They juggled shells and clam surprises,
And sang with joy, to all our rises.

The seaweed waved in quirky cheer,
As sea horses fumbled round in beer.
A crab made jokes that brought applause,
While fishy whispers held a cause.

Frogs borrowed boats and roamed the bay,
Riding on a sunbeam's ray.
Giggling squids wrote tales so grand,
On pages made from golden sand.

So if you sail in silent bliss,
Keep an eye for a fishy kiss.
With every splash, a funny play,
In stillness found, bright laughs at bay.

Echoes of Silent Waters

Beneath the hush, where silence clings,
A ticklish clam plays on the strings.
He strummed the tides and made them laugh,
A concert held for fish's gaffe.

Starfish danced to tunes so sweet,
As penguins flopped on dabbling feet.
With jellyfish in hats so bright,
Their disco lights filled up the night.

An octopus played hide and seek,
While laughing lobsters jammed all week.
They shared their funny tales of grace,
In water's arms, they found their place.

So flash a smile when all seems still,
For laughter hides where dreams can fill.
In silent depths, there's joy to glean,
With every giggle, nature's scene.

Subtle Rhythms of the Deep

In hidden depths where bubbles swirl,
A shy fish fluffed its fin and twirled.
It dreamed of becoming quite a star,
A comedy act, not seen from afar.

The anglerfish wore silly socks,
Trading gags with sea-bound rocks.
While nameless critters acted shy,
But burst with laughter, oh my, oh my!

Anemones danced in gentle tides,
Their wiggly moves let giggles glide.
While narwhals formed a choir so odd,
Singing tunes of joy to the sea god.

So float along where laughter rings,
And join the fun that water brings.
In subtle rhythms, find your beat,
With chuckles swirling—so upbeat!

The Art of Stillness

In a boat made of marshmallows, I sit,
Hoping that dolphins might join for a bit.
With a fishing pole made of spaghetti,
I dream of a catch that's light and petty.

Clouds above are just pillows of fluff,
They whisper sweet secrets, all soft and tough.
My heart beats in tune with a jellyfish's jig,
What rhymes with tranquility? Oh, the search is big!

The seagulls are laughing, they're quite the jest,
As I bob on the water in my soggy nest.
I find joy in the still, where chaos should reign,
With each rubber duck, I abandon my pain.

So here in my vessel, I find my delight,
In the ocean's embrace, everything feels right.
Though I might look silly, I'm having a blast,
In this silly stillness, I'll forever hold fast.

Glimmers of Hope in the Abyss

Deep down below where the fish wear a frown,
   I try to convince them to turn that around.
With jokes about plankton that dance in the dark,
   Their scales start to shimmer, igniting a spark.

An octopus tells me, 'What's blue and not sad?
   A fish that can't remember! Isn't that rad?'
I chuckle with dolphins who laugh at the tide,
   In this underwater circus, we're all on a ride.

The starfish join in, they're doing a dance,
   With moves so absurd that I can't help but prance.
Glimmers of hope twinkle from seaweed so green,
   Reminding us laughter can hide in between.

So here in the depths, I wear my best grin,
   For even the squids know how to let joy in.
With bubbles of giggles, we float through the gloom,
   In this raucous world, there's always more room.

Oceanic Reverie

I dream on a surfboard made out of cheese,
As sea turtles gossip and dance with the breeze.
A crab named Fred tells stories so bizarre,
About how he once wrestled a giant guitar.

Pelicans wear hats made of jelly and jam,
The ocean is brimming with laughter and spam.
I ride on a wave that sings just for me,
While whales do impressions of silly marquee.

The horizon stretches a canvas of blue,
I paint with my laughter, a splash of the hue.
An octopus juggles, a clown in disguise,
As sea urchins giggle and share in the prize.

So here, on this whimsy, I float and I sway,
In an ocean of chuckles, I dream the day away.
With giggles like bubbles, the world seems just right,
In this oceanic reverie, joy takes to flight.

Underneath the Surface

Beneath the sea surface, where odd fishes play,
A starry-eyed clam sings the blues in dismay.
He lost his top hat in a swell of the tide,
Now a seahorse jokes, "Let's turn the world wide!"

The water's a mirror reflecting our smiles,
As we dance through the currents in fantastical styles.
A whale in a tutu performs with such flair,
While a snail does the worm without a single care.

Coral's a canvas for our little parade,
With crabs acting as bouncers, making the grade.
A dolphin recites poetry ripe with delight,
While jellyfish glow softly, illuminating the night.

So here under surface, we laugh and we play,
In our aquatic world, worries drift away.
With humor as current, we float through the fun,
Finding treasures of joy in the light of the sun.

Reflections of Peace in Saltwater

Seagulls squawk like old men,
Arguing over fishy gems.
The sand tickles my wet feet,
As I dodge the crabs on their retreat.

Turtles paddle by in style,
Flipping flippers and a smile.
'We're just here for some sun,' they say,
While sunbathing without a care today.

A dolphin jumps and splashes loud,
Stealing laughs from the ocean crowd.
He flips and flops with such delight,
Making fish friends take flight.

The tide rolls in with a soft cheer,
'What's better than a splashing beer?'
We gather shells of humor and sun,
In this comedy of salty fun.

The Quietude of Starlit Shores

Under stars that giggle bright,
I ponder if a clam can bite.
The moon throws shadows on my toes,
As the tide gives me silly woes.

A crab tap dances in the sand,
Consulting with a puzzled hand.
'Are you my friend or just a foe?'
I shrug and say, 'Let's put on a show!'

The ocean chuckles, rolling near,
Tickling the sand with salty cheer.
I whisper jokes to the sandy floor,
Where shells echo laughter galore.

With each splash, a burping wave,
I wonder if fish can be brave.
Laughing 'neath the starlit dome,
In this serene, silly foam.

Serenade of Resetting Tides

The tides come in with a laughing swish,
Grabbing my toes like an eager fish.
I squeal and dance like a silly child,
While sandcastles stand tall, but it's wild.

A starfish lays down with a sigh,
'Life's too short for a salty pie.'
With every wave, it wiggles around,
Belly flopping on the happy ground.

Seashells cluster like gossip queens,
Whispering tales of ocean scenes.
'Who wore it best?' they start to debate,
While crabs silently judge their fate.

The tide whispers jokes to the shore,
'Why can't clams keep secrets anymore?'
As giggles wash over this sandy stage,
The ocean laughs, signaling the next page.

Silence Whispering Over the Abyss

The abyss murmurs a quiet tune,
With seaweed dancing like a cartoon.
Fish flip-flop, wiggling so spry,
Debating the flavors of a pie.

An octopus juggles shells with flair,
While a walrus snores, without a care.
'I think I'd like a beach hat,' he dreams,
As dreaming sea critters burst at the seams.

Small waves giggle as they scroll by,
Forming jokes with foam and a sly eye.
They whisper stories of things they've found,
Like old shoes that washed up on the ground.

The silence shared with comedic charm,
As creatures plot without alarm.
In this peaceful, quirky ocean floor,
Laughter echoes, forevermore.

Ripples of Serenity

In a pond where ducks do quack,
A frog jumped in, made quite a splack.
The ripples laughed, tickled their feet,
As fish danced around, in pure, silly beat.

A breeze caressed the lily's hat,
While turtles surfed like pros, imagine that!
They flipped and flopped, a comical sight,
As dragonflies joined in, oh, what a flight!

A snail slid by, quite late to the show,
Claiming it beat the croaking crowd, oh no!
In this quiet realm of peaceful glee,
Every creature grinned, carefree as can be.

As sunbeams joked about doing the twist,
The pond threw a party; you can't resist!
With laughter echoing, filling the air,
Who knew tranquility had such a flair?

The Stillness Beneath

Beneath the surface, fish play tag,
With bubbles popping, that's a real gag.
A crab wearing shades, struts with great pride,
While seaweed sways, doing a silly slide.

An octopus danced, with eight floppy feet,
In rhythm with shells, quite the goofy beat.
A pufferfish puffed, trying to be grand,
But got stuck in a bubble, oh, isn't it bland?

The clams just chuckled, their pearls gleaming bright,
As sea urchins laughed at the silly sight.
In this stillness, where giggles abound,
Even the starfish wore smiles underground.

So if you're ever feeling quite blue,
Dive in the depths, there's fun waiting for you.
The calm holds its humor, a jest so sweet,
In the ocean's embrace, life's silly heartbeat.

Embrace of the Ocean's Breath

The ocean sighed, and in came the foam,
Tickling toes, as if asking you home.
A surfer misplaced, launched off his board,
Splashed into laughter, all joy, no hoard.

A seagull swooped down, for a snack quite bizarre,
Snatching a sandwich from under a star.
While children built castles, not quite so tall,
Dune-combing dreams, in their sandy sprawl.

The tides played coy in their dance on the shore,
Throwing fish tales that few could ignore.
With each little hiccup that saltwater made,
The beach was a stage for the laughter parade.

So ride on the gale, let the breeze be your song,
In this silly realm, you just can't go wrong.
The charming embrace of the ocean so vast,
Will tickle your spirit, this joy's meant to last.

Harmony in the Silent Sea

In the silent sea, where the fish debate,
They'd giggle and wiggle, should we celebrate?
A dolphin insisted on playing the flute,
While pebbles chimed in, oh what a hoot!

Anemones swayed, in synchronized style,
As they welcomed the current with a silly smile.
With whispers of laughter floating like foam,
Even the jellyfish felt right at home.

Turtles shared jokes with their gentle glide,
As starfish giggled, no need to hide.
A crab pulled a prank, pinching so light,
Everyone chuckled, what a lovely sight!

In this harmony, laughter never sleeps,
Where secrets of joy are the ocean's deep keeps.
So dive in with zest, let your worries all flee,
For the silly secrets of the silent sea.

Azure Serenity's Touch

In the sky, a blue balloon,
Floats away, playing a tune.
Fish wear shades and dance on sand,
Clams clap hands—it's quite the band.

Seagulls strut with a silly flair,
Cracking jokes without a care.
Sunbathers giggle, trying to tan,
While sunscreen slides off, oh man!

Paddles splashing in a fight,
Who knew wet games brought such delight?
Crabbies cheer from their sandy throne,
Tickled by the tide all alone.

As the sun dips, a wave of cheer,
Even the jellyfish gets near.
With laughter echoing through the night,
Azure dreams take serious flight.

Soft Hues of the Evening Tide

The horizon's painting a goofy scene,
Pink and orange, like jellybeans keen.
A turtle's tripping, trying to race,
While waves gossip in a bubbly embrace.

Seashells chat, what a blabbermouth,
Saying, 'Head South!'—they're heading out!
Each grain of sand grins as it lands,
Counting the laughter from beach-goer bands.

Flip-flops flop with a joyful beat,
Chasing each other, what a treat!
Crabs in bow ties, waving hello,
Ready to dance, stealing the show.

As twilight blankets, fun hugs the shore,
Even the tide can't help but roar.
Life's a game, and we're all players,
Soft hues invite us to be slayers.

Calmness Cradled by the Shore

A sleepy otter wears a hat,
Lazing about on a mate's old mat.
Sandcastles crumble, laughter ensues,
As the tide plays peek-a-boo blues.

Lifeguards nap, while seagulls squawk,
Plotting to steal your lunch, they mock.
Beach balls bounce like they know a joke,
Rolling us over, what a poke!

Surfboards giggle, waiting in line,
For a splash dance at half-past nine.
Fishy comedians tease from below,
Throwing seaweed while putting on a show.

Sunsets wave—a fishy retreat,
As twilight's serenade feels like a treat.
Wrapped in calm, we share our glee,
By the shore, where we all want to be.

Nautical Dreams of Stillness

In a boat made of butter, we float away,
Sailing through marshmallows, it's a cozy day.
Little fish giggle, playing peek,
Paddling happily, with antics unique.

Dolphins dance in fun-loving sprays,
Chasing the sun through the hazy rays.
A crab in a tux winks as he glides,
While shells tip their hats, full of pride.

Seashells chorus, a sweet serenade,
Blues and greens in a playful cascade.
Seagulls in tuxedos making a fuss,
While beach-goers sit back and discuss.

As twilight whispers soft lullabies,
Stars pop open like curious eyes.
With nautical dreams wrapped in delight,
The ocean's humor glows through the night.

The Serenity of the Swaying Sea

Seagulls dance like clowns on a stage,
Crabs do the cha-cha, they're full of rage.
Shells are silent, yet whisper, a jest,
Nature's comedy, at its very best.

Bobbing boats play tag in a gentle breeze,
Fish tell tales that make sailors wheeze.
Tides lie low, taking a nap,
But the sun yells, 'Wake up! No time for a nap!'

Children giggle while building a crew,
Sandcastles rise as if they knew.
Each wave a joke, with splashes so sly,
It's a comedy act beneath the blue sky.

As the horizon stretches, we all join in,
A sea of laughter, we cannot thin.
The tides may ebb, but the smiles stay bright,
Here in this humor, life feels just right.

Melodies of the Calm Coastline

Rhythmic splashes tickle the ear,
Like fishy musicians, always near.
Seashells chuckle, each one a star,
Making waves at their own bizarre bar.

Crabs in tuxedos march on a spree,
While dolphins juggle with glee by the sea.
Sandpipers tap-dance on sandy stages,
Their little performances spark laughter through ages.

Paddling ducks quack like they're in a play,
Making waves of giggles throughout the day.
Oceans hum tunes with a twist and a shout,
As if they know what it's all about.

When the sun bows low, and the sky's aglow,
The horizon chuckles, but it's just for show.
In this comedy set on the coast's own beat,
Life dances in rhythm, where humor's complete.

The Stillness Within Endless Horizons

Amidst the calm, a fish winks with glee,
It's plotting mischief beneath a tall sea tree.
Squids scribble letters in an ink-bled spree,
Writing jokes that sail off, just wait and see!

Mermaids giggle, tails in a twist,
With all of the bubbles, they can't resist.
"Let's make some waves!" they sing with delight,
Crafting giggles that twinkle through the night.

Clouds overhead look on with a grin,
As the sun sets down, let the fun begin.
Every horizon holds laughter in store,
In this stillness, there's always room for more!

The tides hold back their laughter so sly,
They peek at us with a shimmering eye.
In this grand ocean, let hilarity rise,
Where humor bubbles like stars in the skies.

Radiant Calm After the Storm

The clouds retreat, like shy little elves,
Revealing a joke shared by seas and shelves.
Puddles reflect laughter scattered around,
As nature chuckles with a joyous sound.

Raindrops have ceased their playful dance,
And now the sunlight takes a chance.
Fish peek out, with a grin so wide,
Joining the fun, they cannot hide!

Sandbanks rise, with stories to tell,
Of the tempest's mischief, it knows quite well.
Sunny smiles spread across the shore,
As crabs crack jokes; it's a spirited roar!

So let the breezes whisper and tease,
With every tide, they'll do as they please.
After the turmoil, and laughter is found,
The sea sings softly, a joyful sound.

Meditative Waters

In a pond where frogs do sing,
A duck watched as I tried to swing.
It quacked a tune, a silly beat,
While I flopped like a fish with two left feet.

A turtle surfaced with a grin,
Said, "Jump in, buddy, don't be thin!"
I pondered deep and perhaps too long,
Then belly flopped, and sang a song.

The fish applauded with a splash,
"Look at that guy, what a crash!"
As bubbles rose, and laughter flowed,
I left my pride on the damp road.

But with every plop and every splash,
I found my joy in this silly clash.
No deeper thoughts, just giggles rise,
In nature's pond, where fun complies.

Emblems of Gentle Breezes

Breezes tickle with whispers soft,
As squirrels dance, leaping aloft.
A breeze came through, my hat flew high,
I chased it down with a comical sigh.

The trees all laughed with leaves that shimmied,
"Hey buddy, look! Your style is skimpy!"
I tossed my cap, then joined the play,
In a foolish jig along the way.

A butterfly waltzed, quite the sight,
While I stumbled and took flight.
Spinning around like a top in glee,
As pollen danced with me in spree.

In that moment, the world was grand,
With breezes tickled by clumsy hands.
Such folly in the air, so light,
Who knew nature could spark such delight?

The Peaceful Horizon

I sailed a boat, or so I thought,
But found my dream was poorly caught.
The wind blew hard, my snacks took flight,
Pretzel crumbs sprinkled a silly sight.

Seagulls swooped in, a crafty lot,
Snatched what I had; who would have thought?
They circled above with laughter and screech,
While I waved them off and started to preach.

The horizon winked like a playful tease,
As I leaned back, rocking with ease.
"Catch me a fish!" I shouted with flair,
But only caught air and some wild stares.

Yet there I floated, a master of none,
With giggles echoing under the sun.
In tranquil waters, my ego did sway,
But at least I found joy in a wobbly way.

Subtle Undercurrents

Beneath the surface, fish start to twirl,
While I attempt a graceful whirl.
I slip and slide, and down I go,
Creating a splash with a mighty show.

The crabs all chuckled, clapping their claws,
"You call that dancing? Give us applause!"
I grinned and twirled with silly cheer,
While starfish laughed, "What's this? Oh dear!"

A jellyfish bobbed with a wobbly flair,
Sang a sea-joke that danced in the air.
"How do you catch a slippery fish?
Just throw in your line and make a wish!"

With laughter around and bubbles aglow,
I splashed with glee, the fun did flow.
In this ocean of joy, where currents play,
Each funny moment brightened the day.

Silken Drift of Silent Waters

In the calm of the bay,
A fish yawned, then swam away,
A crab gave a sideways glance,
While seagulls performed a dance.

Floating like a feathered log,
A turtle sipped on morning fog,
Fish played leapfrog near the shore,
I laughed at their aquatic tour.

The sun lounged on the sea's face,
As jellyfish found their slow grace,
A clam blushed at a starfish's joke,
And waves giggled with every poke.

So let your worries drift like foam,
Here in nature—we're so at home,
With laughter echoing through the blue,
Just nature's giggles—nothing to rue.

The Art of Ocean's Embrace

In the tide's gentle lap, it seems,
A dolphin practices its dreams,
Belly flops, it takes quite a dive,
Who knew that fish could also jive?

A seaweed hat on a lazy crab,
Looks quite snazzy, no need to grab,
Starfish get jealous, try to trend,
Fashion tips from the sea we send.

The pelicans spill their feathery chats,
As otters play twirl with the hats,
Fish roll in laughter through bright coral,
And seagulls perform their best moral.

Yet underneath, the octopus sighs,
"I wish I had better disguise,"
But no one cares in this fun-filled plight,
As fish laugh and brunch is a delight.

Searching for Solace Within the Tides

At dawn, the ocean grins so wide,
Seagulls take their morning ride,
A clam, dreaming of flight one day,
Yells, "Stop! I'm my own ballet!"

An old whale hums a silly tune,
While barnacles dance with a spoon,
The starfish giggles at the sight,
As all creatures join in the delight.

A jellyfish floats with a bounce,
While fish in tuxedos gossip, pounce,
"Did you hear about the crab who flew?"
They chuckle beneath the sky so blue.

With each splash, worries drift away,
Here, no reason to feel dismay,
Just laughter echoing through the tide,
In this world, let joy be our guide.

Radiance of Peace Under the Sky

The shore throws a low-key party,
With seashells dressed up all smarty,
A fish wore a tie made of kelp,
While crabs swayed as they would yelp.

Fluffy clouds in a light parade,
Wave back to the seas as they wade,
Dolphins flip with a splashy spin,
As laughter bubbles up from within.

Anemones sway with delight,
"Who needs sleep when we have night?"
Stars twinkle loud, shells clink in time,
Even the waves feel in their prime.

So nestle in this salty cheer,
With each giggle, troubles disappear,
Let the ocean be your grand café,
Where laughter's menu holds sway each day.

A Sanctuary of Salt

In a haven kissed by the breeze,
Crabs dance while seagulls tease.
Sunburned tourists in all their glory,
Tell tales of past beach day story.

Sunscreen slathered, but still a sight,
Fins flapping, much to our delight.
Sandcastles crumble, the tide gives chase,
Laughing children run wild with grace.

Here the jellyfish float in a muddle,
While fishermen use nets as a cuddle.
The sun dips low, sky painted in pink,
It's hard to leave when all you do is wink.

So grab a snack and hold your drinks tight,
We're at the beach, and all feels just right.
As dusk falls softly, we hear the call,
Of the ocean's laughter mixing with all.

Where the Sun Meets the Sea.

Where the rays dip low for a golden embrace,
Sunbathers sprawl like they've lost a race.
Beach balls bounce with a pop and a cheer,
As clumsy surfboards crash, it's crystal clear.

Sandwiches squished in the damp, warm sand,
Seagulls dive in hopes of a hand.
Whispered secrets between fish and shell,
Here, even crabs can giggle and swell.

With ice cream drips and a sunscreen fight,
Kids run amok, taking joy in the slight.
The waves roll in, each curl a delight,
While laughter and splashes make everything right.

As the day fades, a bonfire ignites,
Ghost stories float along with the nights.
In the glow of flames, with faces aglow,
Sunset's canvas, a comedic show.

Whispers of the Ocean's Breath

The tide rolls in with a gentle whoosh,
Turtles chase gulls in a funny swoosh!
Starfish lounging like they own the place,
Bikini-clad dancers giving it grace.

Watermelon seeds fly through the air,
Splashing the lifeguard with flair.
Flip-flops flapping like wings of a bird,
While beachcombers shuffle, it's absurd!

Sand dollars whisper of days gone by,
As beachgoers flop like fish out to dry.
The lifeguard snoozes atop his tall chair,
While puddles form under sunbathers' despair.

With shells as treasures and laughter in tow,
We cherish the moments like waves in a flow.
So here's to the ocean, the laughs, and the sun,
In this quirky kingdom, life's pure fun!

Gentle Caress of Serene Tides

Oh, what a splish with each playful splash,
As flip-flops fly and the children dash.
The lifeguard shouts, 'Keep your feet in the sand!'
But giggles erupt as the kids take a stand.

Dolphins peek up, with mischievous winks,
While beach umbrellas sail like sailing kinks.
A crab in a shell thinks he's got it all,
Yet tumbles down with a helpless call.

Sunburned noses and sunscreen galore,
Picnic lunches littering the shore.
Frisbees are flung, with the grace of a duck,
While dogs chasetails, just yearning for luck.

As the horizon swallows the day's bright ball,
We sit on the sand, sharing stories with all.
In this haven of laughter, let's dance through the night,
For nothing is funnier than life in moonlight!

A Quiet Halcyon Evening

The squirrels are gossiping quite loud,
As I sip my tea, feeling proud.
The sun dips low, a golden spread,
While my neighbor's grill ignites my dread.

The cat seems to know just where to nap,
Dreaming of fish and a sunny lap.
I chuckle at shadows that dance and frolic,
In this gentle night, life feels symbolic.

A frog takes a leap, but lands on my shoe,
And I wonder what else it could possibly do.
As laughter surrounds the mellow breeze,
I ponder if crickets are just bad at tease!

In this blissful frame, I make a toast,
To the calm and the chaos that I love most!
With friends all around and snacks galore,
Even the nighttime can't make me snore!

Still Waters Beneath a Painted Sky

Beneath the canvas, colors blend,
My brush in hand, I shall not bend.
A duck in a tie quacks out a trend,
While the fish in the pond plot a wry amend.

The sun with its blush begins to wink,
As I spill my drink and rethink.
A toad jumps in, thinking it's a race,
But I'm just here enjoying the space.

The breeze brings whispers of pastry dreams,
As I chase butterflies, or so it seems.
The swans roll their eyes, so prim and proud,
While I teach them how to dance, loud.

With peace in my heart and antics in tow,
I'm an artist of laughs; let the good times flow!
In the stillness of night, we'll giggle away,
As stars join our story, night turns to day.

Embracing the Softness of the Sea

The shores invite with whispers and cheer,
As jellyfish float, bystanders appear.
I try to swim, but seaweed's a cling;
It seems to have found me amusing to swing.

A crab walks sideways, with great finesse,
He's got a style that I can't suppress.
In the shallows, sandcastles proudly stand,
Though mine crumbled fast; thanks, wind's a strong hand!

Seagulls convene for a feathery chat,
With opinions on snacks and the size of my hat.
As I wade through water, they dive and squawk,
Are they mocking my splash, or just trying to talk?

The sun hangs low like a toddler's draw,
As I throw my arms out, am I beach royalty?
Here's to joy in silliness, and soaking up glee,
In the softness of shores, let's just be free!

Horizon's Soliloquy of Calm

The horizon smiles, a cheeky delight,
As kites fly high, testing their flight.
A penguin in shades takes a stroll on the sand,
While I ponder if he has a band.

The wind whispers tales of sea and lake,
While I sift through shells, making a mistake.
A clam tells a joke but it scoffs and it's shy,
"Did you hear about crabs? They can't even fly!"

With sunsets that twinkle, I listen for glee,
And the ocean remarks, "You're the life of the spree!"
Turtles flip off as they take their own run,
I can't help but laugh; oh, this day's been fun.

So here I will stay, where the silliness thrives,
With giggles and smiles, my heart truly dives.
As the stars take their places, one by one,
Life's grand performance is filled with much fun.

Celestial Dances on Water's Edge

The sun wears shades, it's quite a sight,
Dancing on waves, in pure delight.
Fish join the party, with a silly splash,
Even the crabs are breaking out in a dash.

Seagulls are gossiping, squawking with flair,
"Did you see that dolphin? He just did a hair!"
The tide rolls in, with a playful nudge,
While sandcastles tumble, we laugh and judge.

Oh, the starfish giggles, as it tries to crawl,
While kids in the sand are having a ball.
The surfboards wobble, the beach is a show,
With sunscreen dancers, it's a comical glow.

As twilight approaches, the fun doesn't cease,
The moon brings a glow, a silly peace.
So come grab a drink, or a snack to munch,
Laugh with the sea, in this hilarious bunch.

The Calm Breath of the Tides

The tide rolls in, like a sleepy cat,
Snoozing on pillows, imagine that!
Pebbles tuck in for a cozy night,
While crabs shuffle home, in dimming light.

Can you hear that ocean? It's whispering jokes,
With puns and riddles, it happily pokes.
Seashells hold secrets, they chuckle so sly,
As dolphins do flips, they just can't deny.

The wind struts by, in a feathery dress,
Waving to fish as they get in a mess.
The moon on the water is laughing, it seems,
As stars share their dreams, in twinkling beams.

In the calm of the night, let your worries float,
On a buoy of laughter, like a candy boat.
So sit with the sea, in this silly parade,
Where the joy of the ocean never ever fades.

Illuminated Stillness of Twilight

In the hush of the evening, the sea starts to snore,
While the sun packs its suitcase, heading for shore.
The dolphins are yawning, with flippers at rest,
And the sandman's catching the big fish's jest.

Stars twinkle up high, wearing goofy grins,
While waves play tag, they're the silliest twins.
The rocks giggle low, as night draws near,
With candles of light, they spread pretty cheer.

A starfish jokes, "I'm stuck here all day!"
While a clam shouts back, "At least I can play!"
Oyster pearls shimmer, they're laughing so bright,
In the glow of the twilight, what a foolish sight!

Underneath the moon, where the water does glint,
Creatures of the night share a whimsical hint.
So bask in this laughter as day turns to night,
In the calm of the sea, everything feels right.

Drifting Dreams in Seafoam Bliss

Floating through dreams, on a surfboard of cream,
Where the fizz and the foam make a bubbly theme.
Mermaids are singing, with off-key delight,
As sea turtles dance in the shimmering light.

The jellyfish jiggle, they're jelly with joy,
While they whisper sweet secrets to every girl and boy.
An octopus winks, with a wink and a swirl,
"I'll juggle with three shells, come give it a whirl!"

The sand's feeling cheeky, it tickles your toes,
While the waves bring in laughter, as the summer wind blows.
Seagulls are stealing a wisecrack or two,
As they squawk out their jokes, just to hitch a ride through.

With dreams drifting softly on seafoam so light,
Join the fun of the ocean, sway in the night.
In this dance of delights, we twirl and we spin,
Where laughter and joy are a sure way to win.

Gentle Murmurs of the Celestial Sea

The sea tickles toes with playful glee,
As crabs engage in a wild spree.
Seagulls squawk, a comedic song,
While jellyfish tango all night long.

Fish put on a show, a splashy display,
While dolphins decide to dance and sway.
The sun grins wide, a golden smile,
As beach towels fly, adding to the style.

Invisible mermaids giggle nearby,
Trading secrets that make seagulls cry.
Sandcastles collapse with a humorous thud,
As the tide rolls in, it's pure, silly fun!

Under the stars, the moon takes a peek,
While crabs in tuxedos all start to speak.
Laughter echoes through the night air,
A delightful scene, with jokes to share.

Floating Dreams on Ocean's Surface

An octopus dons a hat made of foam,
While turtles play tag, away from home.
Seaweed waltzes with the gentle breeze,
As clownfish giggle, swimming with ease.

A big whale sings a giddy little tune,
Bubbles rise up like balloons on the moon.
Starfish applaud with their five-pointed hands,
While sea cucumbers just make strange plans.

Flip-flops fly off in a gusty swirl,
Caught in a whirl as the mermaids twirl.
Time here is silly, a light-hearted jest,
As silliness rules, putting hearts to the test.

Driftwood giggles on the sandy shore,
While sea urchins serve snacks, asking for more.
Dunes laugh loudly with each little bounce,
As sea critters join in a dance they announce.

The Melody of Feet in Sand

Sandy toes dance in a playful jest,
As beach balls bounce, never taking a rest.
Seashells whisper sweet secrets so sly,
While kids build towers that almost touch the sky.

A hermit crab peers out with a grin,
Though his shell is way too small to fit in.
Footprints tell stories of joy and delight,
As laughter spills over into the night.

Picnics are funny with seagulls on duty,
Who snatch sandwiches—a crime that's quite snooty.
The sun flops down with a rosy, warm hue,
As kids run around, chasing dreams in the blue.

The tide rolls back, revealing a show,
Of sea stars and laughter that continues to grow.
With driftwood as props, the beach is a stage,
As characters act out each whimsical page.

Secrets Safe Beneath the Waves

Clams chuckle softly, sharing their finds,
As dolphins flip high, with nimble designs.
Octopuses whisper in colors so bright,
Crafting silly stories into the night.

Angelfish giggle as they swirl around,
Playing hide-and-seek, never to be found.
The coral reef sways with a colorful sigh,
A tapestry woven where laughter won't die.

A sunken ship hides treasure galore,
But only holds secrets that make fish encore.
The currents carry tales of whimsy and cheer,
Creating a world where it's fun to be near.

While sea urchins strut in their prickly parade,
Each step they take is a new escapade.
In this watery realm, life's a humorous spree,
With laughter and joy bubbling up from the sea.

Nautical Serenity

A boat appears with a muffin in tow,
Sailing the sea so happily slow.
The fish wear glasses, reading their books,
While seagulls gossip and share their looks.

The lighthouse flickers, a disco light,
Dancing with jellyfish all through the night.
With every swell, a giggle erupts,
As seaweed hosts a party, sea critters huddled in cups.

The captain spills tea while adjusting his hat,
A crab cracks jokes under a pearly white spat.
Ocean's a comedian, waves one-liners,
The horizon chuckles, with no sign of timers.

So let's ride this ride with giggles galore,
As dolphins twirl, ever ready for more.
In this vast ocean, laughter's our creed,
The fun never ends, indeed, indeed!

Solace in the Blue

A whale now sings in a voice that's quite grand,
While turtles spin tales of a treasure so bland.
Octopuses juggle, juggling pearls in the air,
As crabs clip coupons, without a single care.

A dolphin walks in wearing shades of hot pink,
While starfish debate if they need more ink.
The patches of seaweed curl up for a laugh,
As fish learn to dance, each doing their half.

The sea cucumber's plotting a heist with a grin,
Stealing the spotlight, and maybe your fin.
Seashells tell stories of parties long lost,
In this underwater realm, fun's never the cost.

With each splash we hear giggles and cheer,
As sea critters toast with their kelpy root beer.
In the calm of the blue, humor floats free,
Life's just a jest, come sip from the sea!

Calm Amidst the Storm

The clouds gather round, looking grumpy and gray,
Yet here's a fish, surfing, laughing all day.
While thunder booms with its serious tone,
The shrimp are all jesters, in seashells they've grown.

The waves dance like ballerinas in skirts,
While the lobster's the judge, in his fancy silk shirts.
Lightning strikes humor, igniting a chuckle,
As the seaweed breaks out in a raucous shuffle.

A pirate ship sails, though it's anchored nearby,
The captain's dressing up like he's ready to fly.
His parrot, a comedian, tries out new jokes,
As raindrops form puddles, birthing puddle folks.

Even in tempest, the fun has a means,
With jellyfish flashing, like disco machines.
In the calm after chaos, the seas softly glow,
Making jest of the storm, as soft breezes blow.

Crystalline Clarity

A crystal-clear day, but the fish have a plan,
To hold a grand meeting, a council of clan.
Anemones serve snacks in their floral attire,
While the clownfish are jokes, and the guppies are higher.

They gather in giggles under sunlit skies,
With sunglasses on and mischievous eyes.
Each bubble they blow pops with laughter and cheer,
A festival of folly brought forth by the sphere.

The hermit crab checks with a clipboard of dreams,
Says, "Let's file a report!" All the coral just beams.
A starfish recalls tales of legends and lore,
As everyone chuckles, then yells out for more!

With clarity sparkling like jewels on the sand,
The sea pure and funny, like life's gentle hand.
In this underwater realm, humor reigns true,
As laughter and solace weave bright shades of blue!

Tranquility's Embrace at Sea's End

A turtle paddles slow with grace,
Wearing sunscreen on its face.
With sunglasses perched upon its brow,
It shakes its flippers; look at it now!

A fish in a bowtie swims on by,
Throwing a bash beneath the sky.
"Come join," it quips with playful glee,
"Let's dance and wiggle – come see me!"

Seagulls squawk in merry jest,
A pelican dressed in a fancier vest.
"Feathers on fleek!" they all agree,
In the brilliant sun, under coconut trees.

With laughter echoing on the breeze,
The sea is buzzing with shrimp and bees.
Who knew such fun could float on the crest,
In this silly ocean, we are all blessed!

The Horizon Calls for Stillness

A crab in a tutu prances near,
Twirling around with naught a fear.
"Come watch me shine; I'm quite the star!"
While doing the cha-cha, it's raising the bar!

The dolphins leap with silly flips,
Dressed in bowties, they dance and dip.
"Who needs a ship?" they quack and chime,
When we can party, and have a good time!"

The sun sets low, but not too sad,
As jellyfish jam, it just adds to the mad.
With neon glows, they rock and roll,
Under the starlight, they yield control.

So come along on this joyous ride,
With every splash, let laughter collide.
In this wild kaleidoscope of cheer,
The horizon laughs, come one, come near!

Calm Horizons Beyond the Storm

A sea turtle's grin stretches ear to ear,
Complaining of tides and stormy fear.
"Why does the ocean love to churn?
I only want peace and a good sunburn!"

An octopus in a polka-dot tie,
Scribbles "hello" on the wavering sky.
With tentacles dancing, it waves so bright,
"Who said calm means sitting tight?"

A lighthouse stands with a bubblegum light,
Spinning around, what a glorious sight!
It whispers softly to the churning waves,
"Let's host a ball, no fears to braves!"

And as the squid plays the saxophone,
The sea creatures gather; they've come from afar.
With bubbles and giggles swirling in streams,
Together we surf on joy-filled dreams!

The Unraveling of Tempest's Grasp

The clouds roll in, all grumpy and gray,
But the fish laugh loud, "We'll have our way!"
With flip-flops on, they boogie with flair,
"Who needs calm? We're free as air!"

A whale with a monocle swims quite neat,
Sights set on a party, oh what a feat!
"Why worry about those stormy blues?
Let's blow bubbles, and spread the news!"

With anchors dressed in silly hats,
And jellybeans chasing through the spats,
In every dip, and every twist,
They sway through chaos, never missed!

So let the storms come and stir the sea,
We're a jolly crew, just you and me.
With laughter ringing through every wave,
In the midst of the tempest, we'll still be brave!

Echoes of Peace Beneath the Surface

Bubbles rise, oh what a sight,
Fish grinning, feeling light.
Do they laugh? I think they play,
As they wiggle their fins all day.

A clam wearing a little hat,
With a crab that's quite the brat.
They joke about the human soup,
And start their very own parade troop.

The seaweed sways in the breeze,
As the jellyfish do the tease.
Cautious of its squishy sting,
Yet they have them all in swing.

So if you swim and hear a cheer,
It's just the sea, my dear!
Join the chorus, sing along,
In this underwater, goofy song.

The Stillness of the Deep Blue

Octopus with eight left shoes,
Stumbling 'round, it just can't lose.
Trying hard to find a pair,
While fish stop and laugh, beware!

Anemones dance with a sway,
They really know how to play.
Tickling fins of passing guests,
Who giggle while they take their rests.

A turtle wearing shades, so cool,
Says life's not just a swimming pool.
Catching rays under the sea,
He claims he's better than you and me.

But then he trips on a coral sprout,
And we all laugh, without a doubt.
In the deep where stillness hums,
A carnival of joy becomes.

Enchanted Seas Under the Stars

Starfish twinkling like bright lights,
Holding secrets of wild nights.
Dancing with the moon's soft glow,
As giddy dolphins put on a show.

A fish wearing a tux and tie,
Claims he's the ocean's fashion spy.
With scales that sparkle, prim and neat,
He says, 'This sea is quite the treat!'

Seahorses do the cha-cha slide,
While crabs rollerblade with pride.
Every corner hides a jest,
In this playful ocean fest.

So let your worries float away,
Join this raucous cabaret.
For under stars, bright and vast,
Every moment is sure to last.

A Symphony of Gentle Swells

A clam joins in a tune so grand,
While dolphins form a merry band.
Slapping fins to the sea's soft beat,
As sea turtles bop their heads to the heat.

A sea cucumber with legs so long,
Claims to have written a silly song.
'It's a hit!' it giggles, then slips and spins,
Creating laughter as its dance begins.

The hermit crab plays the old sea shell,
While the others join in, ringing a bell.
Their music echoes, sweet and light,
A comical charm that feels just right.

So lend an ear to the briny jest,
Where laughter swims and friendships rest.
In this symphony beneath the sun,
Life is a joke that's just begun.

Floating on Glassy Waters

On a lake so calm, I took a dive,
A fish swam by, said, "Hey, you alive?"
I splashed and flopped, made quite a scene,
Even the ducks laughed; they'd never seen.

My toes paddled soft, like little flails,
While seagulls swooped down, sharing their tales.
A sunhat flew off, like a UFO,
But in this calm chaos, I found my flow.

The breeze whispered jokes, tickling my ears,
As I floated along, shedding my fears.
I called out to turtles, "Let's start a band!"
They blinked in confusion, as I rocked on land.

Each ripple that formed held a giggle inside,
As I navigated through, on a watery slide.
Life's simple bliss, a comedic parade,
On glassy reflections, my joy's on display.

Tranquil Shores of Solace

On shores so peaceful, where laughter's the king,
I built a sandcastle, gave it a ring.
A crab came to visit, said, "What's your plan?"
I replied, "To rule—ever since I began!"

The tide rolled in, took my fortress away,
I yelled at the ocean, "Not my best day!"
The gulls laughed with glee, holding their sides,
While I ambled back, searching for joy's rides.

I found a lost flip-flop, it looked quite forlorn,
Gave it a pep talk, but it just gave a yawn.
Together we wandered, two pals out of luck,
Two mismatched shoes, encapsulating 'stuck.'

Beneath the cool palms, I danced in a whirl,
The sand sticking hard, like a sticky swirl.
But under the sun, with friends all around,
I laughed through the day, where silliness drowned.

Silver Reflections

In the moon's soft glow, I saw my face,
Thought I looked sharp; measured my grace.
But a fish popped up, said, "Buddy, not so!"
"Your hair's a wild storm, let's take it slow!"

The water giggled, rippling with mirth,
As I tried to capture the wrong kind of girth.
With silver reflections dancing on me,
Even the frogs croaked, "What's your decree?"

I chatted with ducks, proclaimed my great dreams,
They quacked back loudly, bursting my seams.
"Let's start a band!" I confidently cried,
But they honked in chorus, "We prefer to glide."

As stars twinkled softly, I tripped on a log,
Sending a splash, becoming a soggy dog.
Yet in laughter and light, I swirled around,
In this mirrored world, pure joy can be found.

Celestial Drifts

In a boat made of dreams, I drifted afar,
Sipping sweet lemonade under a star.
The fish next to me wore a big grin,
Said, "You're quite the captain, too bright for a fin!"

Clouds floated above, like fluffy old friends,
Singing soft lullabies as daylight ends.
But one cloud got cheeky, shaped like a shoe,
I giggled and tossed back a pink rubber duck too.

The sky turned to canvas, with splashes of cheer,
As I tried to paint dreams, my vision unclear.
With colors all tangled, like my last hairstyle,
My masterpiece glared—oh, but, with great style!

The moon winked at me, as stars joined the fun,
Saying, "Keep it weird; we're not done!"
In cosmic ballet, my heart felt so light,
Floating with laughter, on this enchanted night.

The Rhythm of Quietude

The cat on the shore, so still and so spry,
Chases her tail, oh my, oh my!
Seagulls laugh with a caw and a swoop,
As they watch her perform a wet-dog loop.

The sand tickles toes, makes a fuss and a prank,
While sunscreen's a lotion, that got my shank!
I slipped on a shell, and my hat flew away,
Now I'm a spectacle, bright red as a cray.

A hermit crab rolls by with a shell that's too snug,
He scuttles away with a hum and a shrug.
The ocean waves giggle, it seems they agree,
That life's little blunders are grand comedy.

So let's splash about in this shimmering blue,
Where laughter's a language, and silliness too.
With a wink and a grin, we'll dance on the shore,
As the tide pulls us in—who could ask for more?

Lunar Caress on Aqua

The moon makes a face, all round and so bright,
It winks at the ocean in silver delight.
Crabs dance like jesters on granules of sand,
While fish form a chorus, a slippery band.

The tide's a big joker, can't help but tease,
Pulling at swimsuits while the dog takes a breeze.
A buoy bobs along with a comical twirl,
It's hosting a party, oh what a whirl!

Flip-flops do tango, they leap and they bound,
While the jellyfish glimmers, a blush on the ground.
I try to take a step, but trip over my feet,
Now I'm part of the show—what a wobbly feat!

Bubbles of laughter float high in the air,
As the tide whispers secrets and plays without care.
With a splash and a giggle, the night drifts away,
Leaving footprints of humor, in soft sands, we stay.

Distant Echoes of Stillness

In a stillness so quiet, one frog makes a croak,
And the ocean erupts like a daring bloke!
Seashells all snicker, they share a sly grin,
As seaweed does the cha-cha, a dance without sin.

Stars twinkle overhead, with a twirl and a bounce,
The fish throw a party, all gather and pounce.
A dolphin brings soda, with bubbles galore,
"Who ordered this party?" it shouts from the shore.

The crabs serve the snacks on a platter of sand,
While I try to balance a drink in my hand.
A rogue wave comes crashing, and oh, what a sight,
I'm soaked to the skin but I'm laughing all night!

Whispers of giggles ride under the stars,
As the moon takes a bow, with applause from afar.
This magical gathering, with joy in its wake,
Is a place full of fun, where no hearts could break.

Seafoam Dreams

In the land where the sea swirls like cotton candy,
A fish wore a tux, looking rather dandy.
The crabs all applauded as he slicked back his fins,
"Welcome to the gala!" where laughter begins.

The starfish sits thoughtful, counting each toe,
While a barnacle boogies, stealing the show.
A whale sings a tune that gets everyone grooving,
While mermaids play flutes, their bubbly hearts soothing.

"Where's the cake?" squeaks a shrimp in a fray,
A clam throws a fit, "We ordered gourmet!"
But the jellyfish giggles, "I've got something sweet,
Glow candy is tasty! Now everyone eat!"

So we feast under stars while crabs do the twist,
With a laugh and a cheer, how could I resist?
In this dreamy seascape, with joy all around,
We dance through our whims, where happiness found.

Gentle Currents of Calm

In the sea of my thoughts, there's a fish in a hat,
It swims with a grin, and a very big chat.
A octopus juggling while doing the twist,
Catch me a wave, it's a bubblegum mist!

Seagulls are teasing, they dive for a snack,
While dolphins in sunglasses play catch with a quack.
The sandcastles wobble, their towers are lean,
And crabs throw a party, the best you've seen!

So let's ride the breeze on a floaty of cheese,
With giggles and splashes, we do as we please.
We'll build up our dreams, though they might wash away,

In the funny old sea where we all want to play!

When life gets too wavy, just hop on a duck,
And float through the laughter, it's all just good luck.
For in this grand ocean, we're kings of the tide,
With tickles and bubbles, let joy be our guide!

Serene Tides of Reflection

At the shore where the slippers go lost in the sand,
A crab with a mustache strikes up a cool band.
He plays on a shell, 'neath a sun made of ice,
While turtles dance waltz, oh, isn't that nice?

The whispers of fish make a gossiping spree,
Telling tales of a swimmer who's stuck in a tree!
Nearby, a starfish reads poetry loud,
Making all the seagulls laugh out and get proud!

In this bubble of giggles, we float side to side,
With a dolphin who swears he's a skilled water slide.
We'll splash through our dreams with our toes in the sea,
For life is a riot, come swim just with me!

So when you feel low and the waves pull you down,
Just tickle a wave and wear bubbles like crown.
With smiles and a splash, this joy we confess,
Our laughter's the treasure, can't help but feel blessed!

Whispering Waters

In the creek where the frogs wear their favorite bow ties,
They croak out the news with some very sly eyes.
A fish jumps and splashes, oh what a display,
Claiming he's training for the big swimming day!

The ducks in a conga line waddle along,
Singing a quack that could rival a song.
A turtle so wise shares his witty speeches,
While crickets join in with their chirpy little screeches!

Where the ripples do giggle and the pebbles all tease,
We'll float in our laughter like leaves on the breeze.
With game of charades that the otters invent,
The joy takes a dive, oh where did it went?

So come to the bank and let's make a big fuss,
For laughter's the best, no need to discuss.
With whispers of fun in the cool gentle air,
Life's a silly riddle, so let's giggle and share!

Ebb and Flow of Peace

The tide brings a dance, quite the whimsical show,
Fish wearing top hats say, "Look at us go!"
A clam with a banjo strikes up quite a tune,
While jellyfish twirl in the light of the moon!

The seaweed does wiggle in a scruffy old hat,
It sways to the rhythm of the beach's chit-chat.
A pelican stumbles, fish fly through the air,
Landing right on its head, it's a slapstick affair!

So gather your pals for a picnic on sand,
With sandwiches flying, a very fun brand.
As we laugh till we cry, in this watery realm,
We're kings and queens, oh, we take the helm!

When the world feels too serious, come ride on a wave,
With chuckles and splashes, the heart we will save.
For in this grand ocean, the funny does flow,
And peace in the smiles makes our spirits just glow!

Tranquil Breezes on Gentle Shores

A seagull steals my sandwich, oh what a sight,
It squawks with glee, it's quite the foodie bite.
The sun is setting, casting hues of gold,
While I chase after crumbs, feeling quite bold.

The beach is filled with laughter, toes in the sand,
Someone's lost their flip-flop, isn't it grand?
A dog runs by, with a stick twice its size,
While I'm here stuck, trying to disguise.

The wind whispers softly like a cheeky friend,
Tickling my cheeks, it will never end.
A crab takes a peek, in its shell, it's shy,
I wave in return, and it scuttles by.

As night falls around, with a twinkle and gleam,
I ponder my dinner, which was stolen, it seems.
But I cannot fret, the laughter's too bright,
Tomorrow I'll come, with a lunch packed just right.

The Peaceful Heart of the Bay

In a rowboat we row, just us and the breeze,
The water's calm, but my friend has no keys!
We paddle along, making splashes and quips,
While I try to steer, but we're going on trips.

A fish jumps up, and slaps me with a tail,
I sputter and laugh, oh how I prevail!
A picnic awaits by the old willow tree,
But first, we must fix the map, how could it be?

The ducks laugh loudly, what a quirky crew,
My sandwich takes flight, could it be true?
With laughter and giggles, we float out of sight,
This journey itself is a comedy delight.

As the sun starts to dip, we finally land,
With snacks in our hands, oh isn't it grand?
We'll tell tales of today with a gleam in our eyes,
And surely return for more kooky surprise!

Fluid Harmony Beneath the Moon

The moon looks down, with a wink and a grin,
As I flip my kayak, now that's where I've been!
Splashing about, in this watery ballet,
I giggle and gasp, hoping I won't sway.

Stars twinkle above, in the dark velvet sky,
While I ponder my snacks and which ones to buy.
A fish swims by, doing fantastic flips,
Or is that my boat, failing at keeping its grip?

The night air is fresh, with whispers I hear,
A raccoon watches close, giving me a cheer.
As I paddle in circles, I commandeer the night,
Can't decide whether this is wrong or right!

But joy fills my soul, like a treasure to hold,
In the chaos of water, laughter is bold.
And under the moon, in this grand, silly spree,
I find peace in humor, it's just you and me.

Calm Currents of Reflection

Upon the still pond, I toss in a rock,
Ripples dance outward, oh what a clock!
The frogs croak a tune, off-key but sincere,
While I ponder my life with a chuckle and beer.

A turtle peeks out, so slow in his pace,
I race him with thoughts, it's a determined chase.
As the sun drifts down, like a sleepy old cat,
I chuckle to myself, 'Where's my hat?'

The shadows grow long, stretching out like my dreams,
And I ponder my future, bursting at the seams.
Will I conquer the world, or just my next snack?
With a smile on my face, I plan my comeback.

Though serious moments jet past in their flight,
I take joy in the weird, in every delight.
For life's grand reflection is silly at heart,
With laughter as the art, let's play our part.

www.ingramcontent.com/pod-product-compliance
Lightning Source LLC
Chambersburg PA
CBHW072214070526
44585CB00015B/1335